Stories to Read Aloud
to Your Fetus

poems by

Alina Stefanescu

Finishing Line Press
Georgetown, Kentucky

Stories to Read Aloud
to Your Fetus

Publisher: Leah Maines

Editor: Christen Kincaid

Cover Art: Sarah Shields, artwork, titled "Motherdress with red flowers"

Author Photo: Patrick Coryell

Cover Design: Alina Stefanescu

Printed in the USA on acid-free paper.
Order online: www.finishinglinepress.com
        also available on amazon.com

Author inquiries and mail orders:
Finishing Line Press
P. O. Box 1626
Georgetown, Kentucky 40324
U. S. A.

Table of Contents

Stories to Read Aloud to Your Fetus: An Introduction

Acknowledgements

Dedicated to the mothers who did and the mothers who didn't.
To my sister, Carla. To every sister failed by stars and natural bodies.
And to the children we love anyway.

Stories to Read Aloud to Your Fetus: An Introduction

You are preparing to do a wonderful thing. Wonder is undocumented and hard to place. Experts can't even map it. In lieu of starched, well-ironed adjectives, you will discover the cocklebur of unintended adverbs. *Finally* will be frequent.

Wonder aside, this thing you are doing will persist as a memory of what you have done. A memory of what I did while listening to Mozart. A memory of what we did to save our marriage. A memory of what they did to avoid loose vagina syndromes.

No words appropriate what happens to wonder-filled bodies. No shopping lists suffice. No other body seems helpful. A loss is a matter of perspective.

As a result, we have assembled a short collection of age-appropriate stories to read aloud to your fetus. Stories to pour into possible lives. A collection of loves carved into pine bark, promises markered inside public restroom stalls, lyrics disguised as last-minute notes. We know the little gets bigger the longer you bear it. Tuck us into your favorite linen purse. We are not above the fanny-pack. We remain ready to be unzipped and read aloud at idle moments.

Because we know how you feel and how you fail at feeling. We know every parent needs a plan drafted in the absence of mothers. If we are those others. If this is their story.

PRACTICAL MAGIC

Everything is symbol; I myself am a myth about myself,
for is it not as a myth that I hasten to this meeting?

Soren Kierkegaard

Avian Years

I climbed so high I couldn't see the roses. *All the way* is up to a point where pink petal face does not merit an ogle. These eyes ached west.

A wing above the wren's nest is the top of a magnolia, tip swishing left to right. Balance is the burden of mammalian body. Premise being sight.

Eyes wanting more I climbed into the age of avian longing. Skin bare but for what underbrush whispers to unshaved legs. One *hither* never hurt you.

A wing above entered wordless. Bird's eye or mine, I said nothing apart from finger muscle, the groan of a trunk held tight. If grip is a word and not a way above it.

I climb now knowing no word is solid. Eye for an eye, easing, careful. I lick the bark. Hold my breath. Tell the starlings to   give me   the sky.

I Don't Think We Should Use Words Like Meadow Anymore

There is a meadow across from our subdivision which does not belong to anyone. There are no lawnmowers on this meadow where a coterie of crows conduct their general assembly each morning. There is a four-way stop sign but the Stop looks ashamed and some say there is a ghost that haunts the meadow and what the stop sign feels is akin to dread.

There is a crow whom the other crows caw around and he is likely the lead crow likely his name is Frank. There are parents who will not let their children play in the meadow because it is full of weeds and buttercups and fire ant mounds. The parents want someone to own the meadow and develop it. There are many ways to say "develop" without meaning to but there are no ways to say "development" that do not involve the destruction of something else.

There is a child developing their interpersonal skills which means she learns to stop imagining the crows conversing in the meadow. The child will develop beyond freeze tag and when she has developed appropriately this child part will be dead. There is a distinct tinge of ache she will feel when passing the meadow but the pain will be located in a phantom limb. There is no way to discuss the pain we feel in parts of us that don't exist anymore. There is a meadow and and crows and fire ants. There is a place waiting to die. There will be cupcakes and ribbon-cutting ceremonies. There are people who will call the cupcakes an improvement.

Before He Fertilized Us

Do you remember when I laid naked beneath the moon and you called me a scythe? Or that autumn when there was a drought and the only part we mentioned was a splendid sunset? And that joke about a shooting range? And why we danced around the outdoor fountain? My boots more sodden than yours.

Do you remember when you forgot Chopin's Nocturne-in-Something-Minor inside the auditorium with hundreds clapping? Your eyes bulged, fingers frozen. I held the word *impossible* as it slipped from your lips despite the row of fabulous dames whose hair quivered like swimming helmets. You would not let me touch you. I sat on the velvet bench and harkened to toilets flushing. I wiped your mouth and never mentioned how acrid the vomit. Not speaking is different from never remembering. If you do.

Do you remember that bird perched on the rosebush and you said it was your mother? You said the bush was dying as a result of the drought but the bird was an Eastern phoebe posing as your mother. You said it was really your mother because no bird could fake that. You said she would peck you. I placed my palms over your eyes and turned towards the bird. I said I loved you while I winked at your mother. It seemed important to nurture the relationship.

For the Man with A Truck, A Memory

In the backseat, a green nylon gym with racket eyes. Two wristbands you kept as reminders of John McEnroe and maybe Bruce Springsteen. In the seat-back pocket, a receipt you couldn't find from Walgreens,—from that time when you swiped your Health Savings Account card for condoms before learning it was not an approved medical expense.

Just leave it, you said of the singleton soccer sock.

Anything I touched you had a reason for keeping.

You refused to junk the Juicy Fruit gum wrapper. What if Juicy Fruit went bankrupt? The wrapper would remind you of the flavor.

I kept waiting for you to monetize the rationalizations. I kept waiting for a statement about the things you saved fetching good money on Ebay. I kept hoping you'd expand the pronouns of the future to include Us.

We sat in your truck and watched storks build a nest on the telephone poll. You admired the angles of their beaks. If you had a camera in the trunk, you'd press a button and save their shadows.

You tilted your shoulder into mine. To show me the silhouettes of beaks on the cement which could pass for migrations.

The birds came and went. You kept pointing. The motions of leaving and staying bore similar gray shapes.

I was struck by how the storks bickered and pecked while building. And how our beer went flat before going lukewarm. Two incongruences at once might be an omen.

They are something, I said of the storks. I meant to suggest fighting was natural in species who prepared for semipermanent, co-residential arrangements.

If I had a beak, I would have opened it wide and swallowed every shade which stole your attention. If I had feathers, I would have left my best on the truck's floorboard. To hear what you said. To know just once what you saw in me decades later.

We Thought You Were A Flower

We suspected you must be a flower but the sun washed across the windshield at an angle which hid the road from our eyes. What came next was unforeseen. No sweet fetus should be forced to sit in the passenger seat as its father dies. Expiration takes hours. Half of us remained to insist things would be fine. I sang a lullaby about shooting stars as flames swallowed your father. I promised. *Fine.* What a roaming word. The next month composed itself into a series of lines which taught me patience. I got my life in order at the courthouse of coral lipsticks. Bubble-gum could be the gloss or the object of conversation. I tongued the word *accident* until it gave me a toothache. Until the clerk requested a form of photo identification. I could not very well smile and permit the scabs to spill over counter space. There would be hardened blood between us. The clerk's lips clicked like dentures. The clerk had a few questions. "What's in your mouth?" A word. Oh. He stuttered. "It smells like something that happened to me when I was a kid staying at Mee-Maw's house." We agreed on the forest and shameless crows. I said tell me about it. He said it was a long story that ends in a flower. Yes, I said. *I am expecting.*

Before the Demographics of Me Married

1.   I was ambitious, workhorse-driven, singular mother who managed nonprofit programs and discretionary funds. I was free as a towhee trolling suburban birdhouses for brunch.

2.   I co-slept most nights, sex being the stand-off, stand-alone condition. Sex being complicated by the traditional bonds of the Romanian nanny who memorized the blur of your knock's radiant knuckle; crossed herself against the shuffle of single male feet. Nanny mumbled prayers for my salvation. Begged G-d for a spouse to solve me. As Alabama Baptists prayed for my salvation back home.

3.   Both Baptists and Romanian Orthodox choirs united in fear of a female's disgrace. Lording words against the things I did, single-handed.

4.   I wore the same scuffed jeans, recited Seussisms, pantomimed alphabet rhymes. Driven mad with love for a baby son whose nails I bit to keep from cutting. I paid the piper and the Montessori lady and the Orthodox priest to weave his black cassock of beard and incense into holy shields. To prove flimsy tin can talk. The nanny needed to know we were safe from the sins of prior residents. The priest smiled, said he preferred cash.

5.   I paid and paid

6.   thousands that your hands might steal nights to steady these restless hips, inflate these lips with the rub rub rub of beardside stubble.

7.   I paid little given big picture and savings, a count.

8.   Other nights I rented out. Let my head fall over the edge of the mattress, fury of flesh on this tongue. Demographics of those single minutes:

9.   my frenzy, their prayers, tangling with demons. And each gleaming ounce of this body, possessed.

The Fetus That Wasn't a Boy

Once upon a time, before you were born enough to strap inside a car-seat, another fetus shared the same utero-plasm. Scientific fact insists you were not the only fetus to sprout from Daddy's orgasm. Evidence abounds. You spoke to this other fetus in your garbled underwater jibberish which we, your parents, witnessed firsthand at the 4D ultra-violet baby scan party. Daddy discerned the word *travesty* issuing from your rosebud pumpkin lips. Alas, we could not be certain. The other fetus who shared your sac was different from you in its lack of a visible penis. There is much to be said for the things we cannot see but no vocabulary which permits us to say them. I am a fan of the old *Om*.

We your parents, were thrilled by expectation—a baby body and a baby not-boy. Beyond our wildest dreams. The nurse said it might be a girl but she couldn't quite promise anything. She signed away her right to promise under the Patient Privacy Act. We thanked her for her privacy as well as her patience.

We mailed gender-flexible cards with two babies inside a peach bassinet but the fetus who wasn't a boy didn't make it. According to Dr. Undertok, it failed to receive the necessary nutrients and therefore left the womb-nest without breathing a single pipette of oxygen. Dr. Underwhatever said you were a big strapping baby boy because you siphoned all the nutrients from your sibling. Siphoning is different from stealing.

Daddy's eyes spooled with seafoam and bubbles. *What a tough little chap!* Those were his first words about you. Or that's what he figured he'd say if this came to pass. At which point he would also be inclined to confirm if you said the word *travesty* and what the hell he hoped you two might hunt together for countless coming autumns.

The Baby Not Born on a Train in the Arcade Fire Song

I remember every moment of the Marriott. Right ankle blue and swollen from what I'd done in the parking lot hours before. Love is a matter of drinking too much too soon and not saying it. We kiss to the beat of bombs demolishing Baghdad on-screen. Noises I can never turn off. Fall in love with claymation puppets who promise never to die. If love is an eye for an eye, who will revenge us? What should have been a train was a Marriott.

I am married to the man of my best friend's dreams. Married to riding lawnmowers and organic cotton. Married to the softest gray Behr leaves on a living room wall. Married to a poem about Paul Revere he recites given company and conversation torquing towards poetry. You tumble through my belly one million gallops doomed to become a patriot. Giddy-up, I implore. Ride until your thighs shudder and slack. Hold your ground until it bruises. Insist on trains that never stop. Never stop inside a Marriott. Marry the man you kneed on accident. Marry the hands that knead you relentlessly. Marry a song with three simple strophes. Chugga. Chugga. Choo.

Man Watching Woman Waiting

Green mattress, flower-sprig sheets.

What you say: *The city keeps changing. Do you want a beer? Fancy a brewski? I don't know about Sunday. If you loved me.... Stop rolling your eyes, so trashy. Your mother..... Did you see that kid flip his bike? Those were the days. C'mere baby, just come right over here. Don't look so serious. Can you get me a beer? Life is like jock itch. If you loved me....*

Green park bench, violent red tulips.

The scene plays out as expected because you've read the same comics, played the same Sega games, memorized similar psalms in exchange for gold foil stars. Rubberband around her left wrist, bulge in your throat and there you are, running a palm over her tummy and trying not to blush. There, one heart bump away, the middle-aged woman in clementine Spandex, grinning to herself as if she overheard a secret. There is the overflow ashtray. There is an icy father somewhere in a background childhood. There is an urge you have to make this up to her. When she squints shut her eyes and whispers... *There is a baby.*

In the Waiting Room of Stretchmarks

You discover hypotheticals. A screed of alternative facts. A way in which things could be different. You celebrate your pregnancy with a festive divorce. No birds die choking on thrown rice. Friends mud-wrestle for the privilege of toting the divorce papers. Dreaming soon the day of their own division. "I've never been a dyad or a team player." The auto accident renders you even better as a mother. As does meth. You lead the PTA and coach softball. You are honored with blue ribbons for your fabulous life-work balance of addictions. You change your legal name to Devotion. People call you Devout for short. But not in a mocking, nicknamey way. Your skin grows smoother by the hour. You cannot wait to be older. You cannot believe how you ripen into the abundant relaxation of middle-age. All those dreams you never had come true. You are you. However dreamless. Everything you never wanted is evil. A garden of Eden. You imagine a different outcome. Some dream you might have had. If things had been different.

Our First Easter

I stare at the purple dress and try to erase the thought of you in the closet, wearing that funky Jerry Garcia tie. It was Easter and after church. You had been home for two weeks and eager to touch the familiar hymnals. You sang songs but kept silent about Iraq. Anything I needed to know was featured on cable news, you said.

But those people are paid to say things from an official, far-off perspective and I want to know what it was like for you.

I'm no anchor, you said. The skin near your ears was a muddy brown, a dirt sunk deep in the pores, immune to washcloths. Oh let daddy hold the baby, nice church women warbled.

I laid the baby in the crook of your elbow. It was swaddled in light blue and purple resembling a plastic egg. Children hunted eggs in the church basement with baskets dangling from forearms. The baby stared up at you in its unknowing fashion.

The purple dress stares back at me from the hanger.

Your eyelids fluttered above the baby like soft helicopter blades churning a lullaby from air and motion. Then the baby went off. The baby began wah-ing. Wah. Wah. Wah. The baby sirened louder when you dropped it. I tended its wail with sequins of kisses, bright glittering lip marks pressed against its forehead and cheeks, my voice shrill as a party. Wasn't it Easter? Our first holiday as a family? Confetti flew from my vocal chords to celebrate.

You rocked back and forth in the pew and swore you didn't mean to hurt it. Why would you hurt a baby? Why wouldn't the baby stop crying? How could it happen with nothing to stop it?

Shhhhhh, I smothered. Shhhhhh, I mothered you both. I'm no anchor, you swore.

When I found you in the closet hanging from the metal rod, your tie strained towards the ceiling as an underwater rope reaches for the surface, your body heavy, iced, anchor-like. And my hands ruined the hem of that purple dress. The one I can never wear again. Still hanging in the closet.

Counting on You

They are counting on you
to deliver the dream.
You stand
            in surrogate,
heart of steel and froth.
Bubbles and tangles
not your business.
Aim for banter,
hand-made
            brick.

Disbelieve dawn's fingertips
on your cheeks,
collage of limbs to comb,
in the terror of beauty
I spy my collusion.
            Blur
                        of shared blood
      however brief.
The sunset swears
by bad weather.
Mama's hair was lighter than yours
by miles. You bleach
                        black.

Color in your head of a baby crying.
They paid you in passport.
Corporate sponsorship resolves
flesh into citizens. Mirrors
in a mall sell us
American objects.

What if citizens are no thing?
Crowded vessels.
Ships we sail
in our sleep.

BOYS RIDING STALLIONS

What I invaded
has invaded me.

Denise Levertov

A Special-Purpose Fetus

You were totally not supposed to exist since the Bikers for Christ Chief said I was too young to have babies. He had a super-big, movie-style bike which I rode like a running-off Princess. How I laughed when he revved it at red lights. *Faster*, I begged, go faster. *F-l-y.*

I felt like some unwritten storybook girl when he rode that bike off into the sunset and Mom said killing an innocent baby wasn't right. I felt un-storied, raw as half-shell, shucked, shackled, and not understanding what she meant because you were less than a lima bean at the time while I was gearing up for eighth grade volleyball team tournaments. You were impossible yet honest-to-goodness.

That's not on the menu, Mom said. The menu was blank. Nothing to order. People threw questions. I played third base in softball. *There are good lies and bad lies,* Mom said. Then I sprained my wrist on the trampoline. Inside the pocket of the lavender maternity tunic, I kept safe a sweaty, clenched fist. When good lies came out, I pressed my fist against the stomach. You were a speed-bump from the start. You were a lump in the throat slowing feet down.

I stopped brushing my hair and let it grow tangle thickets, fierce bramble-moat no prince could cross. Mom drove to the Jesus Loves Children Center and signed you up to be adopted. By *the Best Possible Family.* I was happy for you because it sounded romantic to be chosen by the Best Possible Family and maybe have your own room with a swimming pool in the backyard. The sales-people made it sound nice and shiny, loaded with barbecues and tiki torch parties. I wondered about sleepovers. Will the lima bean inherit the sleepovers I lost?

The salesperson hummed and said *maybe* sleepovers were a thing in Kuwait but he wasn't sure because he'd never been there. You went to the highest bidder, an emir or something. He liked little girls and you were developing into the right sort of lima. You were going somewhere a salesperson had never been.

Mom verified the check. I suspected God was good for it. *Of course He is good!* Mom patted the hair above her ear and said *God had a plan* for you and *wasn't it a blessing to witness it unfolding?* To see God's purpose working itself out in your *precious little life?*

I wished God would make men's plans unfold faster. Seems God had nothing against listening to folks talk. I prayed about that. I said *Lord. Please. Speed* this trick pony up.

Dragon Gets a Nose Job

is a title you read on the cover
of a self-improvement glossy.

If the dragon wants a girl
we say his
self is wanting.

You are the girl that doesn't get it.

The girl that can't give
up expressive nostrils,
soft flume of early flare.

You stand beneath the skirt
of a solid oak and
the verge is rage.
Strong nose
uncorrected.

Tell the mothers to guard their babies
from the glint
in your eye.

Dragon Does College

You bid for time, bite your tongue. The one true church confuses everything. Parents steward their opinions into elegant lawns. One man's tuft is another man's topiary. Mao is no more than a college dorm poster. A red Che shirt you wear to sleep. In your dream, the heart has its own separate backbone. A linden leaf trembles before and after you touch it. There's one syllable that describes the way you pull a dress over your head. A linden leaf trembles regardless. It's that sort of leaf, you suggest in a way that makes you available. He came, he saw, he yodelled. You bite for time, bid your tongue.

But How Did He Look When You Told Him?

He resembled a man arguing against the temptation of tears. George Washington facing his father over the apple. Hansel trying not to look at Gretel. Malcolm X standing on a playground trying to decide the color of his skin. Walker Percy in a fishing boat with his uncle. Goya at the cross in the chapel. Edgar Allan Poe when the opium ran out and the raven clawed at his brain. A little boy discovering termites in his bedroom floor. William Gass being whipped by his father. Any white-skinned teen who loved a black-skinned girl in Alabama in the 1950s. An eye for an eye, blinking.

Woman Waiting Near the Mobile-Home Window

You don't want to tell him about the money because it seems silly to say it aloud when he predicted it would happen. If he left the cash with you. Things self-fulfill at will. If he trusts you. And you want him to trust you so he will put down the remote and listen when you can't stop saying *closer, closer.*

But it snowed so much more than the forecast and the backyard turned white as your grandma's hair when she was trying to say something—that rattle in her chest, hands slipping from bedside rails like an unhappy baby—trying to comfort you but it came out wrong. "No," she gasped, "I can't die yet..." And then she did. All that white. Not heaven.

You would tell him about the money if there was a way to first evoke the backyard, the table whitened by snow, the four white lumps sitting in hush around it, the lingering peace of a family dinner. You could detail the callouses on ring-fingers given a blizzard to set the table just right.

Lunar Epistemology

A vow is a promise that comes home with shovels and building plans. Of course you wanted to be a puppy from the beginning. A mother knows what she knows without saying. Your grandfather's nose about things which were none of his business. As if it's possible to hide the ashes of burnt crosses from children who witnessed the blaze.

He did the worst his race could muster and then polished his bearings. Those were the Golden Days.

You wanted to be a human as much as I wanted to be some farmer's wife. Who can't even bake lasagna. Unmade for marriage by all the beds in which I lingered. My face was the shellac of stunned. Only force of circumstance can be blamed for the ways in which we are not what we wanted not even once.

Me getting knocked up and unable to procure the pills for mornings—after a man rips off the condom, mid-stroke. My knees piled like broomsticks against the front door. You pelleted inside a human uterus, possibilities bounded by enzymes and egg. A shotgun wedding was all I could conscience.

Let it be clear by the loom of the white-shrouded belly coercion was embedded in the troth. Let it be clear from the pew, smiles sliced across faces are either razors or tiny pistols, the shotgun's heavy sigh, a swishing of skirts, wedded by waltz. It took a gun to make me a wife. As birth rendered you baby not puppy. A mother knows what she knows when the moon makes her say it. Of course things might have been otherwise—my legs wild as kudzu, your puppy heart bouncing, if not for the men who teach us to march.

The Fetus Who Purred

At first, you were mistaken for a kitten by my tabby. Ralph traced your soft, purring sounds with the tip of his pink nose and then rubbed his fur back and forth across my belly. I did not know where to turn unhastily. As the author of sixteen children's books, I ought to know better magic than a couch, a cat, and an ache where once there had bloomed a bright marriage.

Once is a word I use often. My husband spent hours on his phone or computer reviewing porn sites for magazines, industry marketing companies, and men's groups who met in megachurch basements. The tiny console light had gone out. Show me a spare bulb for the automotive console light in a Volkswagen. Our marriage was a Volkswagen at best. Our love reduced to countless pixels which brought in a paycheck yet rendered him captive to rapacious, buzzard-beaked images. I held my arms over my head and protected my eyes from circling raptors. Sex abandoned pleasure for impossible positions, unbewitching facial expressions, variations on the fetid, enjambing childlike thrill with punitive words. He lost interest in sex outside complicated technical contexts embellished by iron maidens, whips torn from the skin of small calves. No tower I fashioned for him to climb was craven enough for the second-hand pornographer, iconographer of the modern billboard era, middle-aged limprod bellyflop, a frog turned froggier by the minute. Add to this a terrifying plot test pronouncing me pregnant. We never planned for children. We lived in yardless condos on purpose. No space set aside for even the tiniest flower bed.

If that man had a thousand souls, I would kill them all. That's what I told the doctor when he asked if my husband knew of your existence. Nothing exists until it becomes a word on the page. This is my registrar. I could not raise you with the help of a tabby named Ralph and deliver your innocent cherub cheeks into the burled arms of the iconographer. I could not plan preschool birthday parties steeped in suspense, wondering when he might find you old enough to be consumed. Oh I could not watch your sweet little brown eyes be eaten alive by the the hands attached to the head ruled by images. In the battle between the icon and the text, my hand forged a reply. I swallowed two pills and bled crimson until all the world's possible children trickled between my legs. If I fainted, only Ralph bore witness.

Don't disenchant your way into a baby who cries. Never mourn the torture of life I chose to spare you. See these words? They are richer than chocolate, warmer than sunshine. See how precious you remain in this head. Forever. *Once upon everytime.*

Girl Watching Patriots Build a Ball

The wall will protect us
from those who came here
outside the law. Those that choose
not to be legal.
Those who imagine they've been given
a choice. A law does not lie
equal across a flat plane.
This land is our land is not
a prairie. Horizon is a view
and not a point of access.

A girl pokes two fingers
through steel ovals.
Metal fence is not enough
to keep her out
of sight out of mind.
A hand is an encroachment.

If power is a line
drawn across a field
to obligate others, I tell the builder
this is my body
he cannot touch.
                    Noli me tangere
and then some. He touches so much
to construct that wall from ear plugs.
Countless cloud-peg iotas.
Clunk clunk whispers the heart
beating along the floor
like a wooden prostheses. *Clunk clunk*
metal key. They have
locked us into a world
made safe by threats.
There is not enough orange
in the sunset's filthy lucre
        to survive
a fiddler's song.

Ode to Pure-struck Cowbell

In a land of cinders and tater-tots lived a lovely maiden who refused to date until she was ready to offer her life to a man she might marry. Alone at the softball game she spotted a man who bore striking resemblance to a prince played by Brad Pitt in her oblong daydreams. Their eyes throttled across bleachers and what maiden faced with such gravity would not blush. One blush led to another and before long they were courting and touching fingers. The man proposed marriage to the maiden at the village's finest buffet. Given the tables covered in steaming dumplings, fried rice, and Mongolian beef, the maiden felt certain she was living a fairytale banquet and this was part of the feast. After the wedding, the time came to venture into unspeakable territories. He beheld the vagina as a darkness infested with bats. Shudders froze him, foreskins of fear and dread. The horror. His stallion shriveled slightly. The wise man's words returned: *One must enter the darkness to discover the treasure.* A story is no story without it. Unexpected events transpire in unlit spaces. The putative prince summoned his courage, buoyed his brawn, mounted his mettle, and plunged boldly into the horrid vagina. At this point, the matri-moaning began. If not for your father's courage, you would never have reached the Sapphire Lake. We would not be making ultrasound maps which anticipate your courageous journey back through the dark, trembly cave. I threw a penny in the mall fountain and made a wish. His name is Lincoln.

And G-d Bless America

Its mild-mannered men
will have cream in their coffee.

Nice suits, neat hair
such gents turn sailor or fascist.

Some die
roll doubles.

I add all this up:
a series of Syrias.

The lie is homeward bound.
The missile made in Poughkeepsie.

Some never leave home
still admire the cloud.

The Farmer's Wife

After Anne Sexton

The windmill changed direction to say you were coming.

I knelt in the grass and parted my legs the way fault lines open themselves to earthquakes.

Tractors bumbled through the fields like peahens hunting absent husbands.

Small fowl seeking florid cock.

Mechanical coos and clucks.

And men building houses.

In the shadow of bowl carved by druid oak limbs, a father rustled.

My skirt fell.

Your face was a natural event left to its elements.

Meadow you call home.

The last thing I glimpsed was a sparrow assembling a nest.

GIRLS WANDERING ALONE INTO FORESTS

"THE QUEEN: You are lying on the pavement, in the street.....There's a crowd of people hurrying by. They think they are going somewhere, but they don't really know where they are going. You cry out. They step aside so as not to crush you, for they aren't cruel, just indifferent. They each carry their own death within them, they cannot carry yours as well..."

Eugene Ionesco

How to Speak Poetry in a Neon Forest

after Leonard Cohen

Remember that your audience is not color blind. Do not read to a room your verbs baste white. A few listeners will snore softly but most faces are awake. In the room you see every color except orange. There will be those who enter a rainbow for relief. There is no rainbow that carries an earnest orange. Appease none. Say no things that illuminate a world without wrongs. Bring the full weight of color to bear on their backs. Hold the paper in one hand and adjust the microphone. The mic is a man you adjust accordingly since Mike must be a male or a tower. Give your name and then blank. Let your mother's ghost brush the hair from your neck. This will be cold. This will be hot. This is a compress. Read slow and steady ochre into the room. Read orange until it rebounds from every face so that a mirror confirms, yes, we are all orange now. Steal the beautiful ebony, the ivory, the gold, the rest, the tan, the pooling browns—no one should cling to a favorite color in the neon forest. Read like the moon's first rave. Of course it depends on the audience. The milieu. The smoking or not sign. No matter where you stand there will be a man in the room with a sister named Taylor that is seriously married to a builder named Matt with a house on a cul-de-sac and two kids playing Minecraft. Taylor and Matt are failing but the kids don't know this yet. Read to Taylor's brother. Then to Matt. Then to poor Taylor. Read as if the children overhear everything. Because they do. When your voice breaks, read louder. Be the 13 year old choirboy whose cracking voice shatters the cathedral window. Don't be sorry. People will pray for you anyway. Read the poem about pews. Flex your knuckles. Erase the text that emerges from naked bodies behind closed eyelids. You can't save them now. Leave them naked. There is time to return after the reading. When you read to the man in your bed, tell him it's just a test. A dry run. A check of engines. Tell him your name and take a deep breathe. He knows the poems by heart. Practice saying your name aloud again and again in a room with a man in the dark.

Inventory for Good Relationships

There is nail polish, a curling iron, this lycra-looking bandage intended to enhance waistlines, an egg dye kit, an IUD, anal beads I bought in Brooklyn, a vase filled with gladiolas.

There is a grocery list on the fridge and his favorite beer at the top.

There is a mold surgical uplift of the sagging breasts.

There is a winning smile and white-as-wedding-dress teeth.

There is a special shade of red lipstick that makes the white brighter.

There is a technique for improving his orgasm which involves sustained digital contact with *eine kleine* chode.

There is a giggle I've got down pat and a cluster-bomb of sports stats committed to memory.

There is the special 900-kilowatt mascara that windows my eyes a little more when he looks like he's craving innocent.

There is a gym membership that keeps my butt doggy-style ready.

There is a cat I pet when the man appears bored.

There is the fact that he's perpetually bored and needy to be watching something.

There is a sill-side sorrow snapped shut.

There is a valiant zipper on a change purse.

There are so many ways to keep a man but not one that doesn't require self-mutilation.

All this keeping is surgical at heart.

The last time I thought about this was in a park where I was holding his favorite green kite, and I was flying that kite for him so he could chug a beer on the blanket when suddenly, an elder-folk jogged past in night-glo spandex and I wondered what would happen if I let it go just like that. I didn't wonder what he would *do*, see? I wondered what would *happen*.

It Was Not the Right Time

I should not try to remember what didn't happen. The shampoo slicking the floor. Marguerite Young in *Miss McIntosh* asking what good we have reaped from electric lights given that we still marry without seeing each other and isn't the darkness best?

Try not to remember the face you made when conversation turned towards fairgrounds. The ferris wheel kept you earnest, palms flushed with coin. A kiss compounded by loose popcorn and the places you wanted to be were not locations but moments in which the arrow pierced the balloon and you liked it so much, winning. Try not to remember the prizes.

Try not to recall one day whiplashed into another, whip and lash, like needle and thread. The studied importance of your feet on the pavement. Intolerance recast as virtue for which I felt guilty. The words written without quotation marks, exquisite. I envied the character safety she found in two old men. Soda pop and teddy bear targets. Men in a story who wanted nothing more than her peace, a plainsong. Peace being the opposite of a pose one offers to others. The opposite of clowns selling balloons with crooked teeth.

I try to look at you and smile. Sex being the opposite of peace. Platinum being the opposite of dark hair layered underneath. Think of the things I dyed to keep from sitting on my hands. Color comes down to this—a body moving across a room fast or faster. A passion flooding the sidewalk like a searchlight, the instep that is not poise but a busk. The wick in me near a ferris wheel busking for pulse that isn't neon.

Give me earthquake over electricity any day. There is no peace in a song I string along, starving. The passion I want is plotless—sharp jags on a line going nowhere, the journey into pulse. A slaking and unslaking. The urgency of what we did in the funhouse. And the walk home, afterwards, lit.

Letter to the Midwestern Artist

I have found a different diner at which to begin my days. You would appreciate the waitress, a high-school dropout not a day over sixteen. The girl slides into a common currency: the slick cash of cuteness. Yum yum she says and licks her bubble-gum glossed lips. This is not a Schiele painting. Not a medieval unicorn tapestry. This is an ad for toothpaste but the girl isn't getting paid.

I should have gone when the giggles glazed over, shiny as wooden icons. When the gold became a fragment of face and not some mystical sacred sheen. I should have gone when the Trotskyist hearts broke in unison—while there was still a bouquet inside the machine gun. While there were still flowers. Still life in the future of a blast. Revolutions might yet have bloomed in technicolor firecrackers. What cracks now is knuckle. The current crackerwork: stilettos over sidewalks. Determined daughters—the girls who are driven—step straight into the open mouths of the cracks. The crunch of their mothers' broken backs.

Before you kissed me, it took a catechism of dirty words to open the hymnals. You admire the prism of our song. I saw panel after panel of stained glass. Not an illusion of optics. The prison bars of long ago beauty real as stares that bleed. True as the ache of icons. The tears tumbling from wooden faces. Women with heads shrouded in black kerchiefs, their steps vague as park pigeons.

I should have gone before you hired others to pick through the laundry. All the clothes hung outside. The things we used to cover our bodies turned into diagnoses. The parts you deemed insolent. The droopy chemise arms. The helpless carapaces of unworn days. The things I saw hanging. The things which stung. And the accusation of loose kisses trembled like lips after the piano recital. Little girl lips. The choir on the cusp of the high note.

I should have gone before the embraces grew specific. To unbear what needed bearing. To admit what had been borne. To know better than the competition. How could I compete with the flesh you froze in monuments?

I should have gone before you presented me with a gift that assumed my death. The stone statue which said I was done. A piece of work. Your product. To know nothing could alter the monument of me. Hard rock being what a materialist makes of fresh-plucked memory.

I should have. Despite the surly awning of yellow daffodils. Despite the pie graph of love on our side. Despite the rules gathered from Nancy Reagan's palmist. Despite the subtle setback of acorn tide which felt almost lunar. Even if it was. Even if it wasn't. Despite the lighthouse and the fog and the face hereafter. Despite the pieces of a script we'd perfected through performance. Despite the boxloads of blazing candles and the slow grist of wax. Despite the yes yes yes. Even if it was a yes. Even if it wasn't. Despite the scent of clover of summer's fingertips and how much came of this and that. Despite the sum of those. Even if there was a calculus. Even if there wasn't. Despite the things you said to make us real, including the lullaby of solid prose used as a bedtime blanket. Despite the binkie. Despite how carefully you covered me. Because you covered me. Even if you didn't. I should have. Gone.

Not Black on the Ultrasound

There is no easy way to spread legs for the stirrups. I stare at the screen, your shadow is black and white, a shape missing melanin.

Statistics screech through my head like breakfast traffic: 10% chance you inherit the clotting disorder; 33% odds of notorious BRAC; 45% likelihood that color-blindness renders your world colorless as your daddy's.

The raised garden beds I tend against tides. I plant tomatoes knowing the risk. The high likelihood one will suffer from aphids. Even after you're seeded, planted, by the book—let's assume 10 fingers 10 toes—accidents happen to change you.

The nurse says the doctor is delivering triplets. I smile at three thoughts together.

The first trees to take hold in a swatch of mother soil are called pioneer trees. This has gone on forever. In our state the white pines were here first. They may never let you forget black skin looks scorched from a distance. But what are the odds of anything? 50% chance that you are an empath

lugging the crosses of sad strangers through lobbies and check-out lines I don't know how you'll manage. How any of us survive. White pines are replaced by red oaks and ash trees, species that thrive in the shade of white Goliaths. One tree succeeds another. A natural progression.

What will the neighbors say when white pines die out? When the natives disappear for lack of sunlight? A planet is a color-driven place. A fact of life may turn out fallacy. A fact of nature may be sheer accident. Forest ecology is perennial pre-existing condition.

One Refugee to Another

Near the railroad tracks where we swore never to cheat again lies a pile of aluminum cans, mostly Coors, a place of promise being another human's dump. I read books about hobos, memorized songs for tamping ties, a track glinting in my head, a solid, steady buzz turned tinnitus. When we hope to minimize the damage, we say it happens to everyone. Is happening somewhere. Now. The manufacture of motive left out too long, rain makes mildew. It happens to everything in the presence of water. Given time. Moisture leaves its mark. I could tell you about the light since light remains marvelous no matter what we do with it—bombs, barricades, spankings, books, pizza. Is marvelous now. Light plays with my head I try my damndest not to touch, all light indicted by association, like church khakis or strobes at a gym dance. Standard horror. Happening now. Later we'll say nothing. Is happening somewhere. Beneath an uncovered bulb. Tender woolen blur of a face undressing in private.

Staring Problem

I stare at the large glass door that does not move. Run my eyes over the floor's silver doorjamb. And the faux wooden handle, unlocked. A squirrel scampers across the porch's two rotting beams. An acorn rolls past soon after. I stare at the door and accidentally observe the squirrel. I scan the space left behind, an absence of squirrel.

Am I staring at the squirrel if my intent is limited to watching rather than staring? Since I find myself staring at the post-squirrel space. Since I think of myself as staring at the glass door. And why does the acorn follow the squirrel when it is the squirrel who wants the acorn?

Carpathians

In the photograph, my eyes track three massive stones. I stand atop a treeless mountain peak with clouds close enough to pocket. Carpathian valleys jambalaya below.

The rocks are named *Babele*, which means old women.

The photo was taken by a Romanian named Vlad I met at the hostel. He told me a story about a boy who froze to death with a piece of ice in his mouth while playing the flute. We stared at one another because the foreign intrigues, the borderlands develop a logarithm of interest.

He asked if I had a thing for spy movies. I did but I don't anymore.

We scaled the mountain to visit the old women. He told me a different story— this one about the first nine days of March in which the statues shed their heavy wool coats. I told him about Groundhog Day. He had seen the movie. It was funny though repetitious.

I stared at the old women as he took my picture. Later that night, my hands felt like ice. As I ran them across his naked back, my fingers stayed cold as glaciers. Had I frozen. Was I solid. Stiff as three old women turned to stone. Or a story he might he tell the others.

I Could Not Explain the Abortion Without Referencing Smaller Things

A dock over a lake. A glimpse of water between lengths of wood. A question about repairs. An absence of particular planks. An ambiguous answer alluding relationships. A motorboat partying past. A remember that time when. A thick, turtlenecked sad feeling. An overcoat feeling. A sense of incongruity between overcoat and summer sunshine on bare feet. A fisherman along the bank looks drunk. A drunk that is ambition. A drunk you discovered in high school. A drunker-than-thou righteousness.

A minnow near the pier. A dock you think is special. A dorkiness remaining ambiguous. A shoulder slouching. A pebble sunk. A plop. A word about water. Another plop. A series of plops like points on a map. A hand trying to hold it. A hand trying to hold you. A hand trying to hold your hand. A tense abdominal muscle. A growl from within a bar. A box which resembles a person. A mirror image in the lake. A hand raised. A silhouette. A third grade portrait project. A shadow puppet. A picture of avoidance. A solid sound. A drunk fisherman may be someone's father.

A father who is missing. A father finding himself in a picture on the bulletin board. A picture drawn to make familiar happy. A happy family sounds like silence. A car on the radio. A special bomb made in Huntsville. A humane weapon. A way to kill people scientifically. A pest control truck. Another hand on your wrist. A beer passed across the tarp. A penis. A kiss. An unordered lexicon. A begging noise. A knee. A dock over a lake. A boy who uses poetry to solve things. A poem that is birdshit on the plank. A found object. A lost feather. A lisp taken out of context. A lollipop wrapper crinkling into a skirt.

A clarification. A cleared throat. An unclear exchange. A combination of clarity and obfuscation. A class you took together. A dragonfly speaking to a sneaker. A subordinate clause. A space between coats in a closet. A word connoting air freshener. A stick of peppermint gum. A dry mouth. A kiss you mistake for a hand. A way of looking at you which rumbles. A motorboat you missed. A boy who keeps waiting. A promise you exchanged for peace. A time when you promised. A time that tasted multilateral. A loss you discovered in high school. A thief who loves you. A thief who loves you. A thief who loves you throwing rocks in the lake. A plop.

Yellow Mama

"Breed, comrade women, it is your patriotic duty."
Nicolae Ceausescu to Romanians, 1984

1.   I was born in a country that doesn't exist. A Soviet Socialist Republic of Romania, known for AIDS-borne orphans and stray street dogs. A Balkan needing salvation.

2.   And so You came. You saw. You selfied. Then planted McDonald's. Clear-cut a culture that left room for weeds. Seeded new scriptures, a sign of the times. In this gnarled heart I know you would have loved Nicolae Ceausescu, Prince of the Anti-Abortion Republic, where monthly workplace vaginal probes were required by law. To check women for babies. To save baby lives while Communist Party fingers invaded a mother's.

3.   Kitchen table abortions automated jail time. Justice was swift and vengeful. To save the embryo. First Citizen of Romania. Land where possession of birth control was punished as illegal trafficking of drugs, a violation of the national body.

4.   I say a man's personal border decides the line between import and crime. You don't believe me. Why should a show dog believe a mongrel? If the fence is a wall sustained by armed soldiers I swear Party Animals smell the same in any geography. The force of flag sweat. For love of country covers everything.

5.   A border is a policed boundary. A custom is the privilege of plundering Others. You are So Party. All Party. Party Till You Pop. Middle class native white bodies your Party is the only one that counts.

6.   In Romania, only Party members were permitted empty wombs. Only the Party ensured flesh against fetus. Official papers. Life can be a blade sanctified by statecraft, a boot on the neck of a beast we think can't really hurt.

7.   Yes, I was born in a land where parents listen to shadows inching over concrete. Shadows don't speak unless you count subtraction, sound sucked away from nearby objects. And what is a woman's silhouette against concrete if not wild meadow, fertile field, unentered mine? What is a mine if not a national resource? What is natural is a resource owned by men.

8.   Bonafide smiles and big ole blessings never believe me. You of the holy-roller heads, empty hearts, blinded blinkers, seek the refuge you won't grant refugees. Keeping busy. Bearing bibles. You keep bringing the bible to the people of Romania. Arrive with a church group, eager to snap a shot. Press send. Tell the world what you've done for Romania. Tell the world

9.   I was born in a land that stopped naming its children Nicolae. The dictator's name curses any child it touches.

10.   The books you avoid still happen. My parents crossed an ocean to be considered aliens. I weave crowns from honeysuckle vines, memorize the native plants your children have forgotten. I read and recite. Some one needs the guts to remember this story.

11.   Here I stand, XX, nurture + nature, watching Christians push petitions to bring Yellow Mama back. Beguiled by the vacant wist of the executioner, his grizzled lament, the retirement of Alabama's electric chair, the Mama you miss most. A mother who kills is native Kali. An electric chair is the proper Southern matriarch, penultimate sizzle.

12.   Don't be fooled by the *portamento lento;* a slowly sliding tone may be Benjamin Britten's scream. Box Merlot may be *passacaglia,* the bass inside my imported belly will never bear your life or win your race war. I stitch lips shut, muzzle vagina, tuck verbs safe inside the sheet music. Bind my body into what is forbidden, what is true

13.   samizdat. I was born in a country that doesn't exist. Yellow Mamas, please keep your pale blue-eyed Jesus in the home-sweet-home stadium. Muffle his face with freedom fabrics, white stars, blue bars you brand across his back.

Terrorista

You call me. I could never tell if the thrill came from sex or sworn secrecy—ideals to enforce, consecutive plots, limited knowledge of who might bear a bomb and where to drop it. The lies aroused us like barefoot tango, couples swirling in circles over crackling parquet floor, a movement away from movement.

I could never tell how to handle the terror of life at war. One builds a bonfire and warms your hands with others. Terror divided loses its power. A horror we share is toothless as the village *baba*. All jaw.

Once I was another girl fearing shadows between buildings at night, the lather of angry male voices. No more. After being raped on the sidewalk, snow piling slow over my face, the weight of frozen water pleating eyelashes, no terror can touch me. There is nothing a man with a gun can take. My feet are a swindle of motion. See. This is a dance.

How Much I Love Your Father

Your father is a gentle man, poet of wind chimes and wilted azaleas. I love him more than verbs allow. My love is an ongoing action, a nest safened by the breast that awaits him.

Emails are brief… he asks about the foster children next door..Mrs. Frangoulis' tomatoes…the rainbows in rust… autumn's first caress… my toe… my heart… is still luminous? The moon is all he recognizes in a foreign desert. In response to my inquires on his health, he writes: "I have been absorbed by certain thought, specifically, the significance of the word 'beloved' as used in the Civil Rights Movement."

Your father did not plan this war. He planned to serve for two years and further his studies in linguistics. He planned to find a secret logarithm that would translate ghazals without losing an ounce of motion. A poem must not be slowed, he said. A poem slowed from one language to another is a crime. The heart beats fast, furious across stanzas.

Your father says less with each email. His voice is clipped over the phone. He is given drugs, drinks, pornography, and army-approved prostitutes—they give me poison, he whispers. Poison to cancel poison. No poem is equipped to metallurgize the shrapnel. It will take years to write the poem which frees us.

Your father is a good man. He meant to hurt no one. This life pains us in places that no home protects. Ambulances ruin sleep with screams of unknown faces. Syntax is sirens in ellipses, a half-beam of flashlight across the wood floor. Please understand. Your father returns in four weeks. His face the vacancy of carnage. Words he must learn and then defend. It will take all of my body to shield him.

He dreamt of you since that iris. The plant he potted and adored. He wanted nothing greater than a daughter. If you know how much he loved you, then you would understand why he will never know of this night. Never know of this decision. Little one, the man returning is not the man who kissed my shoulder weeks ago. He is a ghost. There is no room for babies. What this war has murdered. The eyes wrenched of hope. My duty is to the country we inhabit— the land of husband and wife, the land of black hair and brown faces. Your life, the debt paid down, what a woman offers her country.

Why I Like Complicated Positions

I prefer complicated positions in cramped spaces for sex. Sudden attempts at eye contact make face-to-face fucks uncomfortable given the fleetingness of efforts connecting feelings to specific nerve endings. Which synapse gets fired.

I don't wonder what he's thinking unless he shoves his eyes into mine, intrusive as a couples selfies. A man's gaze is rarely more gentle than his member. He wants something substantial with those fries.

Would I prefer a rear-facing position every time? Generalization is insufficient. A formula comforts, but comfort is the petri dish of boredom. The quantity of comfortable bored folks is clinical. Statistics reveal clusters of comfort coincide with stadiumfuls of unhappy, screaming Americans. The price of comfort is watching a game we're too comfortable to play. Ask me a better question.

Ask me why spooning sucks given my aversion to eye contact. I'll tell you there's nothing as exhilarating as staring long, hard, and deep into his eyes after the thrashing about ceases. I can almost count micrograms of blood rushing back into his biceps and legs, the blood leaving his face, the tender prom-portrait flush, the things he would say if he weren't such a verbally-diminished creature. Ask me why he gets nervous if I get up to go into the kitchen. Ask me why he likes to have his eyebrows kissed, the hair on his back scratched and tumbled like pizza. Ask me why he looks up from between my legs like a little-leaguer who wants you to clap whether he hits the ball or misses. It's not about the ball. Please admit this corruption. It has never been about the balls or the bases or team rankings—only crowds of tired adults rising in metal bleachers to cheer our boy for whatever he's done. Or not done. Same difference. Our boy peers up from my thighs and he believes the applause is coming sure as shooting stars and men on the moon and theatre popcorn. He has earned the roar. Needless to mention his entitlement to the performance of my organs. The pat on the back. He is, after all, the best boy ever. World's greatest grinner. Daddy's little buddy. Mommy's sugar, the cream inside a local bakery's fresh-baked puff.

Free to Choose

The bearded writer asks why we aren't buried in fetal positions.
The monstrous dragon in the garden eats little girls.

We have no taste of Eve
outside Eden. No paradise left to bomb.

I stand inside the white-genocide choir's menu of plans for female bodies.
Weaponized whiteness. Maelstrom of melanin missiles.
In this petri dish news cultures
details into crises. After the fact,
post-truth, past a time when reality is certain
        the Shoah was wrong.

Let's admit how little it matters
        what you feel
so long as people like it on Facebook.

You are free to choose the likable future.
We are free to pay cash for preference.
Free to admire illiberal atrocities.

I know from economics people choose
to believe in monsters for rational reasons.
We think being an ass is an image problem
        not a condition.
Purchase a skinny mirror to see yourself

                        better.
            Manufacture trends dissent.
Fact is a tender social construct,
a skinny mirror for scientists
no such thing as knowing
a subject, no such nerd in context
of Everyone turned expert no such person
outside live-action-womb. We are free to punish
the poorer, shame a pauper after the fact.
We are free to choose one life over another.
Your great tinkle-down economics to
make America bleed again.

Zmeu

The painting of a *zmeu* exhaling fire sits above bed. A *zmeu* is a Romanian dragon. His serpentine tongue is an inflamed roadway, Pentecostal in its reach.

When I stare at the *zmeu* for expanded chunks of time, a tongue of fire slips between the slender window slat, reaches into my room as if the *zmeu* feels my stare. As my eyes are a beckon. He enters as fire and slowly takes the form of naked man who makes love to me and then disappears.

How do I know the flame is a *zmeu*?

Because I have watched one become the other.

Because I have fucked a dragon and let him believe he was making love to me.

Happy Endings

"Learn to predict a fire with unerring precision.
Then burn down the house to fulfill the prediction."

Czeslaw Milsoz

Lullaby for Baby Dragons

I am tucking in the children who
emerged like tiny buds from
my Georgia O'Keefe parts.

The moratorium we put on mothers
comes out cursing. Hurt is not hell.
She saved cursive for holiday cards.

A mother's kiss is a promise that
smells of fresh-cut apples. I hold
her to a scent, a winding orchard

of arms. Miss her scathing scolds,
the scythe shape of love. And how
she cried every time during *Moonstruck*.

My turn to tuck and cluck stories. Leave
apple riddles in a goodnight room. A sleep
tight lip. As wine morphs to blood in mouth.

While All the Handsome Princes Sleep

The moon would be one where a man loved me. Not a man looking up murky-eyed, the stench of coping on his breath, one bar after another may not be a melody. Two children with fever at this hour rising and the solid yellow solstice moon rising bit by bit by digital red dot. I beg my mother to help me. Beg the moon and mind over matter to love me and let me be loved. One man and so many men stiff as shore-stunned starfish, arms snapping off. What is love if nothing when your heart thuds in tiny steps of Fahrenheit? What is life but the story of how I run with the moon, hallowing corpses left on the shore.

The Legendary Fetus-Kick Off

Just after you started kicking—and after my mother-in-law pressed her palm against my belly, squinted her eyes, and declared you didn't kick right—I read a book about climate change alarmists and how they were altering the climate of ideas irreparably.

No one had read the book at the La Leche League meeting. They hardly had time to develop coordinating nursery paint palettes. Life grew a bit much. One fetus kicked like a horse, the other kicked like Tiger Woods, another kicked like a rainforest python, the one to my left kicked like crazy.

There's no right way for a fetus to kick, our La Leche Consultant reminded. But surely there's a way a fetus can win, the one to my left insisted.

We assembled ourselves in two lines on the center of the vinyl carpet. Facing off two by two, belly to belly. The best kicker got to keep standing while the losers sat. No mother agreed to lose. The Consultant stepped in to adjudicate issues of fairness. She put her hand on both bellies to gauge whose kick stuck.

Imagine my astonishment when you, me, the one to the left, and the fetus to the left were the last ones standing. Disbelief when you were declared the winner of the Fetus Kick-Off Contest.

Nonsense, my mother-in-law scoffed. She didn't trust a judge who nursed twins in tandem. *There's no right way to kick*, I informed her. Even though, obviously, you were the best. Don't ever forget you're a winner. Mommy's best kicker and such.

Adjustment to Ancient Legend

She laid in the hammock and imagined all the world's unborn children, hidden in the paisley of her grandmother's long cotton skirt. Remembered a Jewish legend that empowered ejaculate. An uplift for scrotum. When a man ejaculated onto the ground, a little devil came to life. There were millions of such little devils sown by careful, shame-faced men with bulbous noses and worn briefcases. This was why women asked men to come on their face. No demons are born from the seeds a man plants atop a woman's body. And that's why women tend the planet's spirits from atop porn-crusted pedestals. That's how mommies keep devils away.

Great Idea

The idea was to convey a sense of urgency through sensitive slogans. Several had magnets on the back. The idea was to make people think about what was worth sticking. The idea involved vivid, big-tent graphics designed to unoffend gun-carrying types. The idea was not graphic in itself and so a graphic was devised to bear the idea as an image. The idea might be interpreted as apocalyptic by high-income households. The idea need toning around the edges. The tone of the idea was not taupe enough. The tone could use a muscle. Those who spend time with the idea heard it howling. The howl of the idea could not be reconciled with its uplift-style graphics. Children liked the idea when it was conveyed in stories. Teenagers liked the idea when reading it in comics. The medium-is-the-message was a different idea in dialogue with the idea. Marketing teams transcribed this dialogue into bullet points. The idea did not include bullets. Some felt the points were bullet-like in their precision. The distance between the idea and its bumper sticker required silence on the question of bullets. Proponents of the idea liked points and considered the value of compromise. Opponents of the idea wanted the tent to include concealed-carry types. The idea looked different at sunset with a glass of merlot and fireflies. The idea looked good in pants and certain rompers. The idea did not look good in bikinis. The idea was unappealing to segments of the population who preferred ideas with ample bosoms. Idealogues worked to build up a sizeable cleavage. NASCAR fans liked the idea in one-on-one surveys but not when it intruded on football. Not when it started talking. The idea looked good when it shut up. The idea started to look tired. The idea was not fresh and could use a touch-up, possibly teal. The idea distracted mothers from housework. The idea kept fathers from mowing lawns and recycling. The idea created barriers to entry where doors had once been open. The idea held its breath and counted backwards. The space between each breath was a face the idea had failed. Over time the idea became a country of defaced persons, a country of headless smiles. What's a *corpus* to do when an idea destroys us.

The Myth We Invented Because You Shivered

The nurse explained that 30% to 44% of fetuses shiver on ultrasound screens. We felt as if she relegated you to prototype, a cliche unbecoming of your unique splendor. Daddy jumped to your defense, citing statistics about statistical inaccuracy in obstetrical outcome scenarios. What was the nurse implying? If you were typical, did that render us ordinary despite the fact that no such thing as normal actually existed?

Daddy was adamant and doing that thing with his nostrils. Did the nurse mean to suggest that we who had fallen in love at a rally defending Planned Parenthood might be construed as a meme? The nurse was reflecting her own beliefs about abortion in the context of an innocent encounter. Had we not defended a woman's right to birth babies as well as not birth them? I was confident in using my body as a shack. But not until it could be considered a good shack, a safe house, a stop on the underground railroad of whatnot.

The nurse's hair frizzed dishonestly. She insisted it was merely an ultrasound we needn't take personally. But you were personal as possible to us from the start. Daddy defended you to the best of his ability. I suppose this was the turning point, the moment in time when we elected to go 100% Montessori.

Post-It for a Partner Who Travels

Romanian fairy tales slaughter children at night. I read *Basme* for comfort but the bed is missing two legs. A four-legged creature with limbs is a slide one tumbles on accident. Shadows tip-toe on stilts. The silhouette of camels against the wall behind the red candle. What is the difference between longing and missing? If we need four legs to sleep. I am writing to tell you first person the paint is peeling from the eaves. A dog is gone. Our terrarium did not take.

The Story Grandma Will Never Tell You

It's not a story for children, my grandmother warns. The mother and the baby both died. The father scrubbed blood from the cracks of the wooden kitchen table. He did it annually and on their saints' days. He raised two little boys alone.

When she says it's too complicated, I assume she's referring to sepsis, blood poisoning, the wrenching death common to back alley abortions.

My grandmother says they ate on that table for years after her death. The father began each meal with a prayer to the "Theotokos," or heavenly body. The boys bowed their half-combed heads.

I beg my grandmother to tell their story. Because it happened to a mother and a wife.

But my grandmother insists people would not understand. It happened under Ceausescu, in Romania. The words sealed off in a mother tongue. Buried deep in an alien language.

Number Games

My kids play with numbers as if they were bananas. Digits being things they peel before tasting—palpation precedes taking to tongue. A child is an open mouth at heart. What's left is a sweet sum of rinds, remainder that falls to the floor like an unshaped story. What lies there is listless. Unsheathed verbs slimy as center-fold fruits. I watch the numbers turn into games. Six uses for a kitchen towel include parading. Six ways to use fabric, one of which is toga. Another pin-up paper doll blanket. An over-the-hardwood sled. These ways in which a game might backfire amount to life expectancy. The games I can't play with numbers keep growing and growing. One day, they'll be gone.

Trucks Kids Count

"The thunder is the sermon and not the truth."
Traci Brimhall

We play fatalistic games which leave us no choice. I don't want to play anymore. We decide to drive. Tender words grumble like empty stomachs. A child who is truly starving lacks the reality of saying so. Tender words grumble and rumble into freight trucks on long black highways. Trucks carry precious cargo. A car goes vroooooooom. Rest stops flock with tingly-legged travelers running from trucks and running into them. There is nowhere to run without trucks. No resting absent tender words. An elderly man in a non-union baseball cap says my husband would not like what I'm doing. A baby nursing my breast on the bench. A husband taking his time in the bathroom. A lonely old man saying *those things are for your husband.* Those things must be my breasts. One must not be possessive about objects. A lonely man forgets what he learned as a toddler. A husband emerges with fresh-washed hands. A curmudgeon asks if this thing is acceptable. A thing includes the breasts as well as the nursing. A breast is a thing at all times, no matter what its form. A husband says it's cheaper than formula. The old man smiles. A good bargain is a thingamabob he gets.

Psalm

For the crochet hook and
      the knitting needle
maker of homes and warm bodies.

For the slender wooden dowel
      that broke inside a
woman no one dared help.

For the raspberry leaf and
      the stinging nettle
boiled across centuries.

For the pliable metal
      coat hangers that
we hid in household closets.

For all who have died
      female bodies
the merciless felled.

Homelands, Pantries, Hallways

> *"...the poet's homeland is his poem and changes from one poem to the next..."*
> Paul Celan

A mall is a traffic jam of smiles corseted by thunder. Kept open by a sun we can't trust. A light burning our shoulders. Did you cry the first time the skin peeled from your back? Inside every word is lonely: what heat does to the body that craves it.

We stay alone inside this commerce. A wooden duck beneath my arm and Paul Celan's promise speaks in red neon, simple exit. A drive home is the hope of a notebook, a roadblock of hugs and hello mommy. If we must write a new home every day, spin a place of return, the effort runs on allegiance.

Enumerate what life pits against homecoming. The healthy breakfast. The early reading series. Cartoon characters can't keep up. Lord of the Rings aloud. What can I swear except pinky? Celan taught me nothing about using a can opener. I lose a tinsel of blood with each can. Every effort costs us a drop of vitality. A morsel of pain. A journey best travelled with eyes shut and arms held aloft. I urge you to ride. Live the poem. It takes the wrench of a massive steel roller-coaster to move something minute as a kidney stone.

Four Children: A Choose-Your-Own-Adventure For Grown-Ups

Four children, one flaxen, one ginger, the other two dark as smoldering embers. They sleep in the same bed, each forming a curl atop the mattress. Four curls that never tangle. How would they grow never sleeping stretched tall? Tell me, how would these small coiling shapes impede their development? Be vigilant, mother. The vigil is yours to invent. Anew each evening, a fresh vigil keeps you bolted to the foot of the bed, eyes fastened to little faces. Imagine the ballet lessons they ought to begin. Any day now, the piano. The pacing back and forth, a rhythm section, bedtime percussions, the lullaby of worry worry what. Four children you have but only three you can keep. Mother, how will you choose? Which of the four will you lose? All the waiting for losers at night. Mothers, fathers, uncles cheering from metal bleachers—all the team spirit held against fright. I am a mother like any other whose allure is counterfeit. Lullabies laced with germ theory. Acting the part until a curtain of nightmares covers me. Four children, I see. Lids closed, shadows streaming. One to lose. A story taking years to unfold. I wander from room to room in my black linen robe I tell you the suspense is killing me.

To You Whom I Fail

I will say things which sink into a hole behind the green
metal toolshed. I will say these things and you will disbelieve
which is to say that I will fail you in unfinished ways.
If I could be a fundamentalist about text and revelation—

To be literal is to a demand a name for things.
A label shimmies like a shoehorn faced with any ole heel.
The shoehorn does not care whose callous. It cannot
acknowledge the existence of non-heels. Anything
in the world that is not a heel is nothing.

A stone skips across the lip of a lake and I fail you
with my maybes. You who discount the existence
of that which cannot be named, I fail you with my
longings, my dolors and dithyrambs, mystery riding
tongue nonstop. Splendid misunderstandings.

Silly girl. You harlot for twinkle twinkle.
You moon for tiny stars. Cancer can swallow mothers
younger than you. And it does. These are facts.
What will you make of the evidence?
Fail them all. Let the tongue of the mother cat
groom you. Let the stars stitch you to sleep.

In My Mother's Pantry

The softball smashed through the glass door. Squirrels abandoned their wrought porch spaces. A feeling of shatteredness pulled me from the sight. I slipped into the pantry, bit my nails, closed my eyes fire-drill tight.

Somewhere a rose shed petals on a tablecloth.

Somewhere a man mowed his mother's lawn and avoided reading his wife's text messages.

Somewhere a child played piano in a mall and imagined Mozart.

Somewhere a girl kissed a girl on the cheek and the world tasted like fire.

Somewhere gas lines leaked into groundwater and quenched the thirst of fetal cells that would be given the name Tyler.

Somewhere a friend was winning a contest I had entered and wishing she could win without facing the awkward good wishes of losers she loved.

If I opened my eyes, canned asparagus spears and chicken broth might surround me. In a pantry.

So I kept my eyes shut and imagined all possible conflagrations. The wish and the bitch and my tongue on the house.

Your Mommy, the Mermaid, the Dragon

"It's not enough
deciding to open.

You must plunge your fingers
into your navel, with your two hands
split open,
spill out the lizards and horned toads
the orchids and the sunflowers,
turn the maze inside out.
Shake it."

Gloria Anzaldúa

Dragging the Mermaid Ashore, Her Hair in My Fist

A swishy green sequin tail is vivid, easy to remember. I delve the distance between a lizard and chameleon. Their eyes are hungry little Cheerios, circle marks I can't answer. One is also the chatoyant other. I aim towards origins. Once upon a time we all start in the same ocean. Sea to shining *me me me*. A painting is canvas at some point eyes carry color outwards. *Have you seen a mermaid mommy?* I'll row you towards rainbows if magic permits. Close those round pumpkin eyes, imagine all the world's mermaids—their slick turquoise trunks, wiggling waistlines, silver lips blowing bubbles mistaken for breath. But then *How can they live without oxygen?* I don't know how or why a heart breaks afresh when moths swarm a streetlamp. Furious batting of wings avails nothing, we get nowhere, despite craning tiny bodies to run our lips across a light.

Moon We Can't Take Back

He said October's first full moon is the hunter's moon. Its fullness still fallow. Promises muttered in its light are not platinum minerals but passing frenzies of color. Dusk's curious quotations. A single bewitchable sight.

A color is not a solid thing. Not a thing which can be broken into component parts on a coffee table. Not history. You married the American with an easy last name. A name that guarantees ice cubes in the glass of soda. The wedding stayed small because you've never trusted those who make a spectacle of belief. Either you believe it or you don't. Cut the cake and hold up a slice. What is trust: the words a person whispers beneath the shade of a sassafras tree. A halo rendered by sunlight. You swear never to say *linden* again. You have killed all the trees which came before him. History begins now. With this twelve-inch gap between the metal and the word. A vow.

The Letter Under the Sierra Club Magnet

The letter is written in red ink on heavy sketchbook paper. The letter says he misses her. The letter says she can't doubt the existence of a house and car and children between them. She musn't rush to judgement for he has the mortgage papers in a manila folder to prove it. Stamped by a notary public. The letter says she should take a deep breath and remember their intense desire for one another. She should trust that desire. She should consider much money they had blown to satiate that desire over the past decade. He has receipts for airline travel to prove it. Some are digital receipts. The letter says she is complicated and not an easy woman. Her parents agree—she is hard to live with—but he is not making excuses. The letter says he misses her so damn much he doesn't know how else to put it. Or where to put the missing. Some way to fill the blanks. And who would have thought empty places get sore over how much it hurts to find nothing there. The letter says the problem with empty places is hope. No place is empty and unexpectant. No empty place accepts its hollow core. Every vase in the kitchen cabinet wants to be filled. But empty is mute—it can't speak. The letter says the problem of missing her is that the part that needs her is a place that is absolutely empty and no sound comes out. She should trust the emptiness because it can't speak unless you fill it a little and then it reminds you of how much more space needs to be filled. The letter says he didn't sleep well last night. He kept thinking about love and the way love's glass is never half full but mostly half empty. She musn't mistake his anger for lack of love. They shouldn't count sheep when their thoughts are full of empty glasses.

Pew Dragon

In the pew where you guise the face of baby-drenched breast, you are their mother, fondled pieta. In the pew where little heads nod as music ekes from aging organ. In the pew to your left sits a friend's sad mother. And another behind. All the mothers we lose to others. All the mothers living has left. Mothers that are not yours smell of concrete. Mothers that are not quite St. Paul's Letter to the Ephesians when meeting their daughter's queer friend. Mothers not yours laughing at little ones. Mothers not yours that know everything about foreign policy except the names of countries, the geography of borders they call natural, the flags they police. Mothers not yours breathing, sighing, sipping Merlot, dabbing lipstick from fresh-bleached teeth. Mothers not yours looking serious, concerned, beloved by someone. In the pew where mothers not yours turn pages, the click of French manicures, the accordion of fingers, tired circus monkeys, long sighs, paper fans. In this pew where you miss the stars and a mother once upon a something, the mother you're becoming, sincerity leaves bruise-marks under eyes where sleep should end things. All the mothers in the world, tired statues. If sleep is a place you find her. If life is to come this is death.

You Said I Could Be Anything

for Lydia Alina, 1948-2015

I search the drawer for a letter,
discarded carnation, a postcard
resembling Vegas.

Some days I am a walrus
that morphs into a fruit fly.
In a house never home.
Where a garbage truck's yodel
gives us dimension.

Some days I am the octave
of Emma Goldman, a skirt
behind a podium conceding
we are all neoliberals now.

I search the shrubs for seed
packet, metal rake, sprinkler.
Some poets douse themselves
in bottled water because it's
hot. I want to feel hotter.

There is a way to wake from a dream
in which you are a casserole.
There is a recipe against dying
young with your head in an oven.
There are cookies to bake
for the play-date.

I have been everything now *Mother
Mama Mommy* searching for socks.

Purple Martins

The purple martins congregate around a collar of guards. Show me the pseudonym for purple. Show me the name purple hides behind when the feather is missing. Not a word without pluck. The pain behind my right shoulder blade careens over sidewalks like drunk stilettos. Sharp edges the croup of a little boy nestled beneath the grayest wing. A man's name is a wing under which all things game-day huddle. A man's name is wing and a ring and something to hide a separate face. Coryell is a nice enough name but my pain is the drunk part. Coryell is a nice name but a name may be a wing when what I need is a port. When what aches is a deviance. A baby that barks, a pen in high heels, a spirit in shin splints, a stumble some mistake for mothering. The last purple was a silk bedspread I left in the dumpster. After you left, the scent of you broke away. A scent wanted to stay. Heartache is not purple but an ache between the blades that burns when I write and burns when I don't. What's damned stays open wide as eyes when a baby barks croupy and the night sucks me in…. at least I have a working pen. At least the pen is a flint that feels like a flight.

Does Each Shoe on a Grasshopper Constitute a Miscarriage?

He said your head hurts.

    She said how do you know?

    He said your face is drawn and the color is gray but also blotchy.

    She said it is almost time to go.

    He said what about your head and are you sure?

    She said we could die tomorrow and what would it matter.

    He said it must be a migraine.

    She said we could die today on the drive to the theatre anything can happen even if it's not what you planned. Even without a ticket.

    He said we've been planning this for a long time and I hate to waste the tickets.

    She said you can put them on the fridge under the Humane Society magnet.

    He said why do you hate animals?

    She said I don't know.

    He said why.

    She said what do you.

    He said if you hate animals.

    She said I can barely see your eyes that's how bad it hurts.

    He said people are animals too.

    She said the pain is like whatchoomacallit behind my right eye and is my head still attached to my torso?

    He said you try to avoid things.

    She said where.

    He said here we are, going nowhere and not the theatre and now we're doing it again.

    She said hurt me.

    He said I can't.

    He said there's too much competition.

    He said what about the baby feral cats run over by cars and have you thought about that?

My Head Is a Harbinger

I told the man he ought not wait for dinner, the old magic aloof.

I loved him for the sex he delivered with pizza. What girl gets through college without going all-in on American men?

I held my hands against the air and told him why not count these fingers.

I hoisted my head onto a pole and said what you see is a harbinger. The lines round my lips going nowhere. The hair matted beyond coconut oil. My eyes two thousand screens irretrievable via upscale remote control.

If I don't wait for dinner, the feminine will have fled from my life, the man said. (—And then Roland Barthes about how the waiting is a feminizing process.)

We are both women now, I told the man. We are ladies waiting for a lover to salve things with sautés.

The sitting position across the white formica tabletop pitted us eye to eye, waiting for a woman. I initiated an arm wrestling match. He lost half the bouts of paper scissors rock.

The man resembled Penelope in her waiting for Odysseus, although one must replace the man with a home-cooked meal. One must imagine a waiting which events us—a weening sort of waiting, the Rapunzel's rapt, tower-like attention.

We attend the gendered distribution of waiting as I subvert its hope. No stove, no ladle. We'll never know what Penelope did since the man told the story. I imagine she had a few lovers to fill the interim.

When is dinner? the man asked. And asked.

I said *wait* for what's looming. A woman might screw you to show the world that she can. If you are a man.

And Eternity

I believe in the crawlspace of kudzu
tiny pockets where we find
forgotten marbles.

Eternity remains an unsafe space
for human conquest. Give us wonder
we'll destroy it.

Progress is so many parking lots
ton upon ton of poured pavement
no surface over which to smuggle light.

Speak to me of sorrow
and I will say Che reserved
his final words for the man that killed him.

"Remember," he said, "you are a killing man."
The executioner complied. Bullets
bound them together forever.

Fruit of My Loins

When they beg, their words turn woollen, thick as horse-hair. Pleas scald the lips like fresh coffee. Little ones beg until the burn begets a blister. What's a good Mommmmeeeee to do? I'd buy them a pony if the purchase bought me silence. I'd pay money to quiet this self. But the pony will need grooming while begs begin again. Now for a puppy. I'll be back at the corner of the driveway staring down the pileated woodpecker assuring the neighbors *no no no no no no no of course not of course this is not a scream.*

Muffin in the Oven

for Heidi

I have a friend who bakes love into torque cake. The last thing I baked was a thick cloud of smoke. A whippet of dragon-breath. Fire leaves a visible vacuum. The sound of my smoke is heavy dragon-gallop, the wallop of mattress to floor.

You say there's a sweetness to savor in fire hazard.

I say *lay then*. Lay on it with me. Where there's smoke then fire is what if not married? What's marital if not thickets of underbrush eager to burn?

If only your eyebrows were paradox by nature rather than poise. If only your poise was simple woodland stubble. The price of clear-cut forests grows slowly.

A muffin in the oven.
                    A napkin on the table
                    folded in my image.

                                        Folded over
                                        so often you
                                        hardly see
                                        the person
                                        in the paper.

If I ask you to describe the person in the image of me, you will say it's only a napkin. You will say others hide in the cabinet near the plastic cups.

But there is no reassurance in a reassuring tone at dusk. As if *only* is ample.

I see how easy to leave love for all the yard's fireflies.
How simple to follow a flicker.....

All Those Love Notes Swarm Like Insects

The note tucked into my backpack pocket.
First note. A simple question with a doodle resembles a turtle nearby. His fingertips rich with Irish Spring. An answer is what begins when all he wants is an answer. The heft of high school hardback textbooks I cannot let him carry. What was the song we sang with car windows open? A lyric hallowed by Cowboy Junkies: *I just want to see what kills me.* That's all I can say. Yet something to lay a brick over.

A note folded under the windshield wiper.
A rose attached. Blood red like a period. Blood is an end to things but male eyebrows are exclamation points. If you're not afraid of anything, then why are you avoiding this? His questions feel sticky—our eyes glued to the slightest change in silhouette shapes. Nothing equals sudden changes in pulse. Equations not learned beneath the evening of words he draws over my face. Luminous. I am glowing. What is bright must be protected from its own reflection. There are things we don't want our friends to see. Kiss me. The moonlight pouring steel from our faces. He can't believe in God but he is grateful—a jig in the streetlight—he has found another belief. He is loaded with what must happen. I am empty of what comes next. The blueprints of first love pure as Soviet engineering; we devise marvelous plans without accounting for equipment. This was Alabama in the early 1990s. A right-to-work state deprives its students of unions. We thought we can make it all work with hands and head.

A note tucked inside a small book of poem by Samuel Taylor Coleridge.
The poems circle love but the note describes jealousy. We hold hands in the hallway so he can assert us aloud. Our friends know I don't date—I am too much the Romantic for humans. The color black beguiles me best. Who are you looking at? He wants all the answers. To touch more parts of me never yet touched. His fear is white, baptismal. I bow my head in service to such occasions.

A note glaring from my car's front seat.
Two dog-toothed violets with hearts for leaves. Words move from love to idolatry. The aromatic incense of ritual sacrifice. I am terrible at proofs in trigonometry. He offer to help—proofs fill his fate. The more he touches, the less he trusts. *You are mine. Are you mine? You are mine forever.* A sentence contains its own counterpoint in the form of intention. I compose myself and lose the

self I love. When I lose control, it is as if a wolf begins panting, a foreign howl which scares him from some dark grave. He says the words enchant at night. He is my first everything, but the more I give, the less pure I become. *You are an animal,* he worries. Animals cannot be faithful.

A note written on the inside of my wrist in black ink.
The Latin is *fides*. A fealty. In the cinema, we whisper through the subtitled movie, reading one another rather than lines. I know French but he can't keep his mind on the subtitles. Unlearning proofs. Popcorn falls to the floor, a pretext to bend down and hide the face. *You are no longer pure so why should you be faithful?* He asks the same questions in car seats and restaurants. This is what happens when you let go. I promise there is no one else. But can I promise there will never be? We have been in the woods at night. Make no promises in the wild. A moon keeps us safe from pure light.

A note etched inside the cover of a journal gifted on our first anniversary.
The love story he has written about us, to keep me in place. I smile at being found familiar. The sweetness gives back the bounce of a jaw blowing bubbles. He loves me too much to trust me. I believe he lies about disbelieving God. Only the devout are taken by signs and portents, the gold talisman he clasps round my throat. A heart I speak for two.

A note beneath my Romanian pillow.
Meet me in the yard when the world falls asleep. I dance in the living room before the floor-length picture windows without knowing he watches. *What were you doing?* The demand of a livid face. A lover needs answers. I was dancing in the dark. *But for whom?* For no one—dancing in the thought of you.

Two notes on the nightstand saying there is no such thing as a thought.
If there is only performance. For whom was I performing? To dance like Salome is to dream a man's destruction. My bedroom walls cloaked in Schiele and surrealists. He sees through the prints. He spies the secrets I am not saying. Begin with graveyards. Begin with the girl who wants to die like Joan of Arc. Save the world but not a boy. You can't save the heart which suspects you.

A note among underwear in my dresser.
Don't forget. I brush the vowels from my hair and stiffen into pillow. Loose-

leafed words lack rubber bands. All these notes he pens to protect me from the hands of another. All these love notes swarm like insects looking to nest. One instant unequals forever.

One note leftover.
A note a man finds later. In the house with a garden and children. A married man who sleeps on the left side of our bed. All beds in which we sleep are left. A man holds the note which grows more serious with time. *See this? I'm not the first one to suspect you aren't mine.* A fear goes back to the beginning. The first kiss and I am unfaithful. From the first to the final note, an echo rings false.

To My Lovers

Jean Follain, I tried to face the animal
but blinked when I saw the billboard.

Anna Swir, I laughed in the Atlantic's face
while choking on the ocean inside me.

Louis Simpson, one white naked bulb
illuminates nothing. We cram our bodies
into dark houses together.

Walt Whitman, the song of myself was stolen
by little ones calling me mother, meaning mammal
lost to autonomous, unique space.

Judah al-Harizi, the mother's lute is beautiful
in portraits. I waited for the painter; performed
appropriated delight. Lies I've posed come back
to taunt me. Speak to me of music without
instruments. Speak to me of the nights.

Wislawa Szymborska, the grain of sand in my stomach
keeps growing. The courier calls from
the kitchen. Who can swear to be human
in a fetal position?

Francis Ponge, give me one *objet-jeu*
for the family road trip. One relief
that isn't acid. Have you written the diaper,
the carseat, the creamed carrot mush?

Denise Levertov, what more must I witness
before absorbing the presence of a pink linen apron,
the smother of unassuming feminine clothes?

Li Po, I cannot go home again. I cannot
devise lyrics to embellish the prison.

Antonio Machado, of course the ride looks
lovely from the window. You are a man riding off
in trains denied me.

Gloria Anzaldua, I will crossroad my heart.
Please Gwendolyn Brooks, hold my hand
through terminal hopscotch.—Joseph Brodsky,
stars twinkle, pillowcase tears, pinchmarks.

Anna Blandiana, whisper my name
in Romanian. It's the only poem
I crave from a grave forever.

Dear Czeslaw Milosz, give me
a border, a beacon,
a bough
            from which to hang
this cradle. Teach me
to rock it. Show me the word
for what happens
when the walls and
the angels tumble down.

Instructions for the Man That Married a Dragon

Tell me stories that might come true. Watch me walk across the bedroom barefoot and imagine a cane in my right hand, the anguish of lies forthcoming. Say we are *fine*. Grit your teeth. Say we are fine but not fine. Devise the last paragraph of any ardor discovered in the kitchen when the kids are sleeping. Cut out all the nouns. Leave only the verbs to move us. Revise the subjects into verbs so radiant all the ardor comes back and leaves us fuckable. Fuck us. Then say you're sorry. *We're fucked.*

Don't point the finger at climate change. Don't reference a cuddle in anthems that rely on the power of words like *majestic*. Tell me the proletariat will have our second car and there is nothing we can do to escape it. Resuscitate the march of history to include battered women. Describe your love for our aborted fetus using words from 1920s psalters. Say you are flummoxed by longing for the way things were. Tell me you want things to be different but similar to earlier. Before you were changed by the round cup of cleavage silhouetted against office chair upholstery. Prior to fake leather chairs and the things we try not to see when someone is talking about grief or diets. What spills out. An image of blood pouring from mom's nose as she died. Explain how blood dries dark at any altitude. It happens to everyone. Tell me it doesn't mean anything except *blood* and *blood* and *blood*. Metaphysics is one way to go nowhere while feeling present.

Epistemology specializes in areas of truth and knowledge. Go ahead. Grow your beard into a blanket. Swallow me with cereal. Devise a diagram to demonstrate how love reduces one's utility function. Draw a flow-chart with eye-batting arrows. Lead me there. Shove my face against the windshield and tell me to look. Say *look baby*. Say *baby look at that*. Once a parent dies, all parents die. Everyone in the planetarium dies. All we have are the faces we preserve in our heads.

Run my fingers over your asymmetric nose and tell me I *love* it. Insist your face will be the one I want to remember forever. The one a funeral will kill. Mow the lawn. Leave the hearth begging for your careless Sunday whistle. Don't hurt the dragon. Leave me begging for the all the blanks you have left.

Wherever We Wander

after Stuart Dybek

Let's dig for water. Bring a long-armed shovel and your mother's dishwashing gloves, cuffs studded with cotton flowers. Rather than radio, you'll hum Jacques Brel, reveal knuckles rich with huckleberry stains, dig-eager hands. We'll nick at the ground and crack jokes about Joseph Smith starting a religion where he couldn't find water. Your laugh will roll me over, laughter rolling through like rural decay, pledging allegiance to nothing.

In your backpack, I'll discover a handwritten note, which you insist is a recipe for cobbler. A recipe in Romanian. You'll watch as I read the recipe I can't fathom. The wind will whisper private thoughts, cardinal directions, signals that won't widen to include me. Shovels fall when you offer you offer a corpulent purple berry followed by your hand, your hand in motion, your hand ambling from thorns to fruit to flesh, soft clamor of kudzu hissing when the breeze strokes its limbs. I'll think this is natural, Envision a vine working its way across a fence, the coils of your body, a pile of dirt, fresh tang of fingers, what we exhume apart from water.

Later, you will stand near the bus stop, the baroque of your long red wool coat, a fugue winding four melodies together—and the chaste trim of your nails will startle me. I'll reach for sarcasm, rueful spark, impending thunder. You'll say don't count the days by their whether. One single wing is proof of a sky.

Change Your Name, Forget the Adoption

"According to Muslim custom, a body must be buried as quickly as possible, preferably the same day, as soon as Allah has taken the soul. In the house of the deceased, we hang a scrap of white cloth from a nail, and it stays there for forty days. At night, the soul flies home and perches on the cloth. It listens to familiar voices and feels glad. Then it flies back."
  Svetlana Alexievich

The man returned from Mosul. The man returned from the gym. The man returned from the sex addiction seminar at the white wood church. The man returned from tennis. The man returned from a gaming convention. The man returned from Home Depot. The baby cried. The baby broke a phone. The baby stopped crying. The baby got a shot. The baby shat on the sofa. The baby cried. Aren't you glad I came back? the man said.

The man said it was nice to be home. The babies multiplied into a quantity of criers. The babies acquired a stomach virus. The man came back from a fundraising event. The man came back from the mailbox. The babies ate carrots. The man came back from the herb bed. The man came back so often I lost count. If you count how often I leave, you will find it is equal with the number of times I come back. The man said this. The man said equal equaled equal.

I felt the equals cancelled me out. The writer said writing was about showing not telling. He showed me his story. In the story, a man came back from fracking in North Dakota. I walked home and imagined stories about women. The women in my stories disappeared. Some never came back. Later the man came back from an office-related social function. I remembered the writer said telling is a turn-off. Torn between wanting to turn him on and off, I made a decision. I decided never to tell. From that day forward, I devoted my words to showing. The babies demanded organic dinner. At which point I slammed the door hard. A song of countless knuckles cracking hit the airwaves as the mirror fell from the wall opposite. It was not a coincidence.

Theories lay on the hardwood, a palette of well-read shards. Even after I crazy-glued the mirror pieces back together, the lines in the image remained. I saw my face covered in cracks. This break is forever. The sun lied. The moon lied. I lied among pieces. Overhead, a flock of something passed.

Sunset In the Graveyard Where I Cut My Hair for Birds to Build Nests

My toddler races through gravestones
a twig gripped tight in each fist
her chestnut bun bobbing, bobbing
& I am the woman trying not
        to lose track of a daughter, a marvel

overhead, triangle of Canada geese
burnished gold. Sun holds wings & feet
in simultaneous formation as oak
leaves fill space between
child and this wild avian.

Please forgive me
the violets
I've trampled
to find you.

Sun, moon, sky, flesh-breath,
may the seasons move us together.
May light sustain within one
singled shadow, a wing singe—
what migrates
cross our hearts
given night.

Acknowledgements

I love you dear mother-tree, wherever you're hiding. I love you precious father, with one hand on every helm. I love you Max, Micah, and Milla—and thank you for giving me space to write the stories of other mothers, to taste the complicated ways in which love plays out within a womb. I love you December for keeping me up all night. I love you barred owl for raising hell with me into the wee hours. I love you Vicki Korner for filling the world with magic. I love you professional self-help books that haven't helped me one bit—thank you for never once helping. I love you Mark Yakich, Justin Daugherty, Sue Brannan Walker, Sarah Shields, Laura Secord, Maureen Thorson, Faith Garbin, Alicia Clavell, Stephanie Anderson Bryant, and all the readers and journal editors that gave these pieces a platform. I love you Alabama, with your terror-torched smiles and sweet tea brigades. I love you American dream for never quite dying. I love you Man In My Bed, teaching me to taste the world I'd sooner torch than accept. I love you fellow bodies tangled by resistance. All of you— all of this—love.

*

Thank you so much to the following journals (and incredible readers and editors) that first published various pieces in this collection, including:

CHEAP POP: "The Letter Under the Sierra Club Magnet"
Cloudbank: "I Could Not Explain the Abortion without Referencing Smaller Things"
Jellyfish Review: "Letter to a Midwestern Artist"
Matrix: "I Don't Think We Should Use Words Like Meadow Anymore"
New Orleans Review Online: "Fetus with a Special Purpose"
New South: The Idea", "The Fetus Who Yearned to Be a Puppy" and "In Your Truck, A Memory" (forthcoming)
Open Letters Monthly: "To My Lovers"
Pif Magazine: "All Those Love Notes Swarm Like Insects"
Profane Journal: "Avian Years"
Red Paint Hill Journal: "To You Whom I Fail"
Spilled Milk: "One Refugee to Another"
Straight Forward Poetry: "14 ways to approach a moon"
The Airgonaut: "Four Children"

Epigraphs are excerpted from the following: Soren Kierkeegard, Diary of a Seducer,: Denise Levertov's poem, "Ways of Conquest"; Eugene Ionesco's Fragments of a Journal, Czeslaw Milosz's poem, "Child of Europe"; Gloria Anzaldúa's poem, "Letting Go"

Additional quotations for specific pieces include:
"Trucks Kids Count": Traci Brimhall's "Sing It to the Lightning"
"Change Your Name, Forget the Adoption": Svetlana Alexievich's Second-Hand Time: The Last of the Soviets

Alina Stefanescu was born in Romania and lives in Alabama with her partner and three vociferous mammals. She is the author of three poetry chapbooks, including *Objects In Vases* (Anchor & Plume, March 2016), *Letters to Arthur* (Beard of Bees, August 2016), and *Ipokimen* (Anchor & Plume, November 2016). Two of her poems have been nominated for the 2017 Pushcart Prize. Her first fiction collection, *Every Mask I Tried On,* won the Brighthorse Prize this year. She remains unbelievably grateful. www.alinastefanescu.com.

www.ingramcontent.com/pod-product-compliance
Lightning Source LLC
Chambersburg PA
CBHW021150090426
42740CB00008B/1033